Dragonflies

Dragonflies

Patrick Merrick

THE CHILD'S WORLD®, INC.

Library of Congress Cataloging-in-Publication Data
Merrick, Patrick.
Dragonflies/Patrick Merrick.
p.   cm.
Includes index.
Summary: Describes the physical characteristics, habitat,
behavior, and life cycle of the oldest insect species.
ISBN 1-56766-381-8 (lib. bdg.: alk. paper)
1. Dragonflies—Juvenile literature. [1. Dragonflies.]
I. Title.
QL520.M36   1997
595.7'33—dc21   96-47042
                         CIP
                         AC

Photo Credits

Adam Jones/DEMBINSKY PHOTO ASSOC: 13
Barbara Gerlach/DEMBINSKY PHOTO ASSOC:10, 26
COMSTOCK/Mike and Carol Werner: 6
Don Garbera/Tony Stone Images: 29
Frank Oberle/Tony Stone Images: 30
Gary Meszaros/DEMBINSKY PHOTO ASSOC: 19
Joe McDonald: 2
John Mielcarek/DEMBINSKY PHOTO ASSOC: cover
Robert and Linda Mitchell: 20, 23
Rod Planck/DEMBINSKY PHOTO ASSOC 15
Skip Moody/DEMBINSKY PHOTO ASSOC: 9, 16, 24,

On the cover...

Front cover: A dragonfly rests on a thistle early in the morning.
Page 2: A dragonfly rests on a reed.

Table of Contents

If you sit quietly by a pond on a warm summer day, you might see many different things. Perhaps maybe a fish will jump high in the water. A fuzzy raccoon might hurry across the beach. And you'll probably see flies and mosquitoes buzzing around in the air.

Soon you might see a colorful creature zooming around with the other bugs. If you watch long enough, you'll see it catch and eat the other bugs. What kind of creature could catch these flying bugs so quickly?

It's a dragonfly!

This dragonfly is waiting for its wet wings to dry.

What Do Dragonflies Look Like?

Dragonflies are a kind of **insect**. An insect is an animal with three separate parts to its body. It has a head, a chest (called a **thorax**), and a stomach (called an **abdomen**). Like most insects, dragonflies also have six legs and two pairs of wings.

Dragonflies have been around for a very long time. In fact, they have been around longer than any other insects. The earliest dragonflies lived about 300 million years ago. They were the largest insects of all time. They measured three feet across their wings! That's bigger than most birds. The distance from one wing tip to the other on a bird or insect is called the **wingspan**.

This dragonfly is hanging from a flower.

The adult dragonfly is made for flying. It's long, thin body and long wings move through the air quickly. To help it see, the dragonfly has a round head that can turn almost all the way around! If you look closely, you'll see that the dragonfly has huge eyes. These eyes help the hungry dragonfly see its next meal.

Dragonflies have huge eyes like this *Green Darner dragonfly.*

The outside of your eye has a curved part called a **lens**. The lens helps you see clearly, like the lens in a pair of glasses. But a dragonfly's eye has 30,000 different lenses! These lenses let the dragonfly look in all directions at once. It can see other bugs moving from very far away.

A dragonfly's eyes has 30,000 lenses.

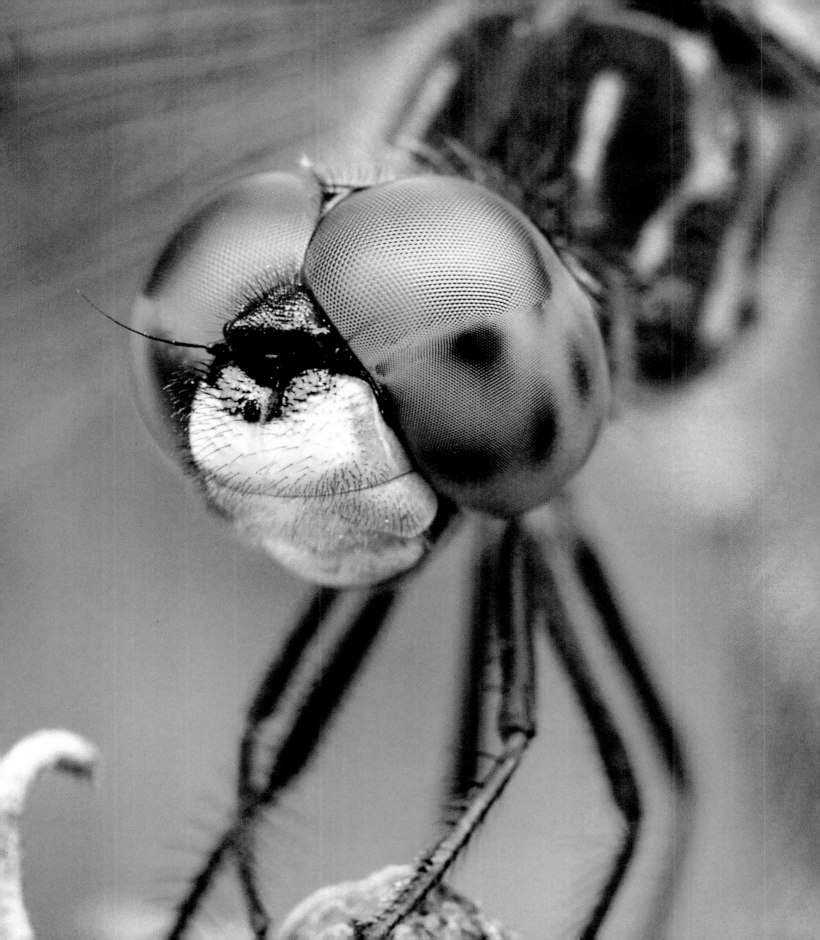

What Do Dragonflies' Wings Look Like?

Dragonflies have amazing wings. Most dragonflies have a wingspan of eight inches, or about as long as your foot. Their wings are made of thin, clear skin. You can see right through the wings! The skin is criss-crossed with hollow tubes called **veins**. The veins carry blood through the wings. Some dragonfly wings also have blue, black, or brown patches.

Dragonflies have two pairs of wings. Each pair can move separately. These strong wings let the dragonflies float in the air or zip quickly in any direction. Some dragonflies can fly faster than 30 miles an hour!

A dragonfly's wing is made of thin, clear skin.

At one time dragonflies were called "horse stingers," "snake doctors," "snake feeders," and even "Devil's darning needles." People were afraid of dragonflies and gave them scary names. They had no reason to be afraid. Dragonflies do not hurt people. In fact, they are a big help! They eat insect pests like flies and mosquitoes.

This dragonfly is resting on a flower.

How Are Dragonfly Babies Born?

Adult dragonflies live for about a year. During that time, the male and female dragonflies mate. The female lays her eggs underwater, in a pond or a stream. A large female dragonfly can lay up to 100,000 eggs in a clump. She needs to lay a lot of eggs because fish and other insects will eat many of them.

After about a month, the eggs hatch. The new babies don't look anything like dragonflies. They don't even have wings. They look like little swimming worms. These dragonflies are called **naiads**. A naiad is a kind of **larvae**, which is a general word for a baby insect. Most larvae look like little worms.

Naiads like this one live underwater.

The little dragonfly naiads are made for living underwater. Their dirty green or brownish color lets them hide. They look like the mud and weeds at the bottom of the pond or stream. They can even change their color to match the objects around them. This ability to hide against their background is called **camouflage**.

A naiad wants to do only one thing—eat. Under its mouth, the naiad has one or two large spikes at the end of a long lip. When the naiad sees something good to eat, it reaches out and spears it with its lip spikes. Then it brings the food back to its mouth to eat.

This dragonfly naiad looks like the leaf it is sitting on.

Do Dragonflies Have Enemies?

While waiting for food, naiads are in danger of being eaten. Fish, birds, and other insects love to eat naiads. Animals that eat other animals are called **predators**. To survive, the naiads must learn to escape from predators. If they are in danger, they swim away quickly. They move extra fast by squirting water through their **gills**, which they use for breathing. Animals that live underwater use gills to breathe.

This naiad is in danger as it sits on a lily pad.

Baby dragonflies can live as wormlike naiads for up to four years. During that time they keep eating and growing. They don't grow like people do, because their skin is too hard and shell-like. When a naiad gets too big for its skin, it sheds it, or **molts**. Underneath there is a new, bigger skin. A naiad molts up to 15 times before it becomes an adult dragonfly.

This dragonfly is leaving its old skin behind.

When the naiad is ready to molt for the last time, it crawls onto a stick hanging over the water. There the naiad molts into a dragonfly. This is a dangerous time for the young insect. It must sit in the sun to harden its body and wings. Until it hardens, it cannot fly. While it is waiting, it is in danger of being eaten by passing birds or hungry fish.

This dragonfly is waiting for its new wings and body to harden.

What Do Dragonflies Eat?

Once the dragonfly can fly, it spends most of its time in the air. It flies around all day looking for food.

Dragonflies are always hungry. Sometimes they drop to the surface of a pond and scoop up a little fish or frog. Often, though, they eat smaller flying insects. They catch them right out of the air! When a dragonfly sees an insect flying, it charges toward it. Then it folds its front legs together to form a basket. The dragonfly uses this basket to catch the insect in midair.

This dragonfly is folding its front legs around a branch.

Today dragonflies live in almost every country. You can usually find them near ponds, lakes, or rivers. They have even been found in deserts and mountains.

So, the next time you are sitting in the summer sun, keep your eye out for the dragonfly. It is truly one of the most interesting creatures on Earth!

This dragonfly is resting just before sunrise.

Glossary

abdomen (AB–duh–men)
The abdomen is the stomach area of an insect. Dragonflies have a long, thin abdomen.

camouflage (KAM-uh-flazh)
Camouflage helps animals hide from their enemies by looking just like nearby plants or rocks.

gills (GILZ)
Underwater animals use gills to breathe.

insect (IN–sekt)
Animals that have a body divided into three parts are called insects.

larvae (LAR-vee)
Young insects are usually called larvae. Dragonfly larvae are also called naiads.

lens (LENZ)
The lens is the curved part of your eye that helps you see. It keeps things from looking fuzzy.

molt (MOLT)
When dragonflies shed their outer layer of skin, they molt.

naiad (NY–ad)
A naiad is a young dragonfly. Naiads live underwater.

predators (PRE–duh–ters)
A predator is an animal that hunts other animals for food. Dragonflies are predators.

thorax (THOR-ax)
The chest of an insect is called the thorax.

veins (VAYNZ)
Veins are hollow tubes that move blood around. A dragonfly has veins in it wings.

wingspan (WING-span)
The distance from the tip of one wing to the tip of the other is called the wingspan.

Index